The Child

Celebrated in Illustration

The Child
Celebrated in Illustration

Text: Peter Bennett
Design: Dreadnaught

A Jonathan-James Book

Penguin Books

Penguin Books Ltd.,
Harmondsworth,
Middlesex, England

Penguin Books,
625 Madison Avenue,
New York,
New York 10022, USA.

Penguin Books
Australia Ltd.,
Ringwood, Victoria,
Australia

Penguin Books Canada Ltd.,
2801 John Street,
Markham, Ontario,
Canada L3R 1B4

Penguin Books (NZ) Ltd.,
182-190 Wairau Road,
Auckland 10, New Zealand

This edition first published
in 1979 by Penguin Books
Canada Limited

Copyright © 1979
Peter Bennett &
Dreadnaught
All rights reserved

Designed by Dreadnaught,
written by Peter Bennett,
in association with BGMRW

Edited by Katherine Koller

Jonathan-James Books
5 Sultan Street,
Toronto, Ontario,
Canada M5S 1L6

Printed in Canada

List of Illustrators

Nancy Ekholm Burkert
Albrecht Dürer
Jost Amman
Hans Baldung Grien
Sir Joshua Reynolds
Johann Comenius
William Blake
Heinrich Hoffmann
Alice Woodward
George Cruikshank
John Leech
Thomas Bewick
John Bewick
Edward Lear
Sir John Tenniel
Ralph Steadman
Gwynedd Hudson

Mervyn Peake
Graham Ovenden
Kate Greenaway
Randolph Caldecott
P. Cruikshank
Jessie Wilcox Smith
Linley Sambourne
Walter Crane
Dante Gabriel Rossetti
Laurence Housman
F. D. Bedford
Reginald Marsh
Hugh Thomson
Tomi Ungerer
Grace Floyd
Jacques Stella
E. W. Kemble

Thomas Crane
Edmund Dulac
Arthur Rackham
Carl Larsson
Maud and Miska
    Petersham
Paul Peel
Thomas Hart Benton
J. and W. Beggarstaff
Florence Hardy
Auzolle
Rudolf Dirk
R. F. Outcault
Harold Gray
Garth Williams
Hugh Lofting
Robert McCloskey
Ernest Shepard

W. W. Denslow
Maurice Boutet de Monvel
Sir John Everett Millais
Maxfield Parrish
William Heath Robinson
Winsor McCay
Walter Trier
Ruth Chrismann Gannet
Francis Tipton Hunter
Maurice Sendak
Mercer Mayer
Victoria Chess
    and Edward Gorey
Heather Cooper
Edward Ardizzone
Norman Rockwell
William Kurelek
…and many
    anonymous others

Introduction

These things usually happen unexpectedly, perhaps while washing dishes in the evening: a reflection on the window pane catches your eye, pulls at your memory and shoots you through the revolving door of consciousness to plunk you on your bed, four years old and holding your hands to the window to see outside in the morning darkness. It is memory and it is imagination, and it is completely unavoidable.

Childhood is reminiscence and imagination: illustration is both put to paper. The evolution of the illustrator's vision of childhood over 450 years is what this book is all about: the blossoming of children and the imaginations that perceived them.

The first illustrations of children appeared in one or two books in the sixteenth century. Although the fire of the Renaissance by then had illuminated many of the passages of the mind darkened in the Middle Ages, children were still seen as small-scale adults. Jost Amman was one of the first illustrators to understand children differently, and tried to convey what he considered the power of their innocence in his woodcuts.

But Amman was an exception, and children remained strangers to illustrators until late in the eighteenth century when a little boy named James Watt disobeyed his mother and discovered that steam from her kettle condensed on his tea-spoon. The Industrial Revolution that sprang from his invention of the steam engine spawned an enormous rise in public education: and that in turn created an unprecedented clamor for books. But illustrations still only filled space on the page, and illustrations of children were no different. Much the same attitude prevailed in factories, where many employees were often less than ten years old.

It wasn't until a teenager named George Cruikshank began penning his frantic, flashing characters that the illustration of children transcended its subordinate function for a final, endless time.

As Cruikshank worked with fussy precision in steel, his countryman Thomas Bewick worked

with equal care on the hard end of a block of wood. Together, for the first time, they brought humor and their own brand of nostalgia to a reader's own memory of childhood. By the time Cruikshank had started illustrating the novels of Charles Dickens, the course of illustration and the place of the child within an illustrator's imagination were altered for all time.

Dickens was a rebel. Enraged by the excesses of the Industrial Revolution, inspired by the monumental pity of William Blake and the romantic poets, his books re-established compassion as an acceptable British emotion. What Dickens did with words, Cruikshank did in pictures: touching, absurd,

full of detail but one drop of sentiment short of maudlin, they created a world at whose center, for the first time ever, was a child.

The result was the cult of childhood and the Arts and Crafts movement that so heavily influenced William Morris, Kate Greenaway, Randolph Caldecott and Walter Crane. To a generation weaned on the fumes of belching smokestacks, a child was the perfect symbol of human innocence of which industrial man had temporarily lost sight. They were the first and last free human beings, and it was not long before artists and writers began looking to children in search of the world's truth.

In the space of a century, something had happened to the human imagination. Material freedom provided more leisure: more leisure led to longer daydreams. And so, while Cruikshank's children clearly lived precariously in a grown-up society, children illustrated in the 1860s and later began to inhabit a world of their own making.

Goody Two Shoes and Lewis Carroll's Alice make this very clear. Rushing about in the late 1700s, Goody is a little girl trying to make amends with the adult world. Seventy years later, Alice shrinks and grows in a land of her own experience, one where playing cards dance and caterpillars smoke opium. For the first time, children were small people rather than miniature adults. They had their own kingdom, their own fears and their own desires. Most importantly, illustrators recognized the child's remarkable powers of imagination.

The expansion of the imagination continues today. Whatever else cannot be said for our strife-torn radioactive times, one thing is true: the imagination is freer than it ever was. Dorothy of *The Wizard of Oz* is to Alice almost what Alice is to Goody Two Shoes: Alice plays in a world dominated by the paraphernalia of Lewis Carroll's drawing room, but Dorothy (a mere fifty years later) occupies an entire kingdom beyond the mundane, a world created by a modern imagination.

Why this incessant drive for larger and more complex worlds for our children? There are probably a thousand reasons, but one of the most important must be the impetus lent by what a child represents: complete freedom to think as one pleases, to live in a world where things can and do happen for no reason at all, where good and bad, right and wrong, up and down just don't exist. Who wouldn't prefer such a place? And there is always the wonderfully addictive attention of children themselves. Kate Greenaway, Jost Amman, Norman Rockwell, Edward Ardizzone and every other illustrator before and after them drew for children, and the sheer desire to please their rapt audiences can be seen in every stroke.

Imagination in its purest form—a fluid line or a little child—should be supreme; can know no limit; is infinitely expandable. This has made selecting illustrations difficult, and doubtless every reader has a favorite that was not represented. In the end, surrounded by piles of books, posters, labels, magazines, stamps, drawings and 'things you just have to include' from a hundred experts, choices had to be made. The criteria were a more open mind, a fresher sensibility and one more reclaimed childhood memory.

PETER BENNETT

Cherubs have adorned paintings almost as long as paintings have intoxicated the human imagination. These winged keepers of divine places flutter through the literature of oriental religions and pose at strategic locations throughout the Old Testament of the Bible.

To Albrecht Dürer, wandering and painting in Europe in the early 1500s, cherubs were men in little boys' bodies, divinities whose immense power sprung from their complete physical innocence (LEFT). Swiss artist Jost Amman's 'Eros' makes these intentions just as clear (OPPOSITE).

Only later, in moralistic cautionary tales like *The Good Child's Reward* does a mask mar that power: this child is more innocent in appearance, more sinister in intent (BELOW).

From simple awareness, thought Johann Comenius, comes complex differentiation. And that is the beginning of knowledge.

Were Comenius alive today he would still find himself in the vanguard of educational reform. The rebellious Moravian bishop was well ahead of his time as he quarreled with his pedantic seventeenth-century peers.

In 1638 he published the first illustrated school textbook so that students might learn to associate words with images. Recognition, he argued, is the first cultivation of the mind.

These illustrations are from *Orbis Pictus* (The World in Pictures). After publication of this book, Comenius became famous throughout Europe and was invited by the governments of England and Sweden to aid in the reform of their school systems.

The illustrator who created the woodcuts, alas, died without recognition.

Sixteenth-century art had a place for children as ornaments or allegorical symbols; otherwise they were ignored, relegated to play cameo roles similar to those of the tormenting 'Stimulants' in Hans Baldung Grien's 1510 masterpiece, *The Drunken Silenus* (LEFT).

Sixty years later Sigmund Feyerabend published Jost Amman's woodcuts (RIGHT & BELOW) of some very adult-looking children in *Kunst und Lehrbuchlein* (Book of Art and Instruction for Young People). For the first time children were central characters in illustration.

From there it was a long jump to the highly moralistic cautionary tales of the late 1700s. The copper plate engravings of *Elements of Morality* (1791) are exquisite (OPPOSITE), but the sentiment certainly is not: this was a book to keep children in their places, and nearly a century would pass before anyone heard another peep.

The trouble with any cautionary tale is its insistence on a world where everything points in the same direction: well-intended or not, rigidity undermines spontaneity, the fiber of a child's soul. 'Don't play with fire,' from an 1817 edition of the chapbook, *The Lily* (ABOVE & RIGHT).

'Little girls should never climb,' from *The Daisy* (ABOVE). 'Don't slide down bannisters,' or your fate will match that of Jimmy Sliderlegs, a Struwwelpeter or cautionary character from the 1850s (LEFT & BELOW).

Sir Joshua Reynolds had no need of text to make a point in his painting (OPPOSITE). Child, obey God.

Three more plates from *Elements of Morality* (ABOVE & RIGHT). The text is classic propaganda that plays havoc with a child's natural inclinations. A fragment from *Elements*: '…if I had not obeyed…I should have fallen out of the coach, and the wheel have gone over my head, arms and legs – Yes, dear father, *while I live I never will disobey you.*'

And if all else failed, there was always the threat of a dying mother to instill conformity now for conformity later (ABOVE RIGHT).

Blake engraved and published *Songs of Innocence and Experience* between 1789 and 1794 as an angry response to child labor abuses (laws were not introduced until 1802) and an increasingly industrialized, dehumanized Britain. He left us a profound exploration of the seemingly contradictory states of innocence and experience. As Blake understood the dilemma, you are innocent only so long as you are unaware: unless divine, you cannot have your innocence and understand it too. Human childhood is an ineffable state out of which we must all tragically pass, and to which we must all try to return. In the frontispiece of the series (LEFT), a child urges a shepherd first to pipe, then to sing, then—alas for innocence—to write down his songs for posterity. The soft, unfocused children of Innocence contrast with the sharply defined, more concrete children of Experience (OPPOSITE).

An illustrated tale with a message, *Slovenly Peter* is perhaps the most durable and imitable of childhood images. Peter's lesson has a distinct Teutonic quality. The original *Slovenly Peter* (LEFT) was written and drawn by Heinrich Hoffmann, a doctor at a German lunatic asylum. Peter's female counterpart, Struwwelsüse, is groomed (BELOW). The story, the

theme of which is the evil of scruffiness, was created for the benefit of the doctor's young son. Since its initial publication in 1844, the parable has been distorted and adapted to suit a variety of societies, including those of Great Britain and the United States.

At times the moral is simple vigilance against disarray, but on other occasions it rises to active vengeance against the urchins who would dare to be disheveled and begrimed.

But always the original Teutonic point is kept: the path out of anarchy is paved with discipline and detergent.

In his modern British version (RIGHT), *Winnie-the-Pooh* illustrator Ernest Shepard depicted a simpler anarchy. He was much less authoritarian than the anonymous illustrator of the first British Struwwelpeter tale (OVERLEAF LEFT). In an early American version (BELOW & OVERLEAF RIGHT), education is the only answer.

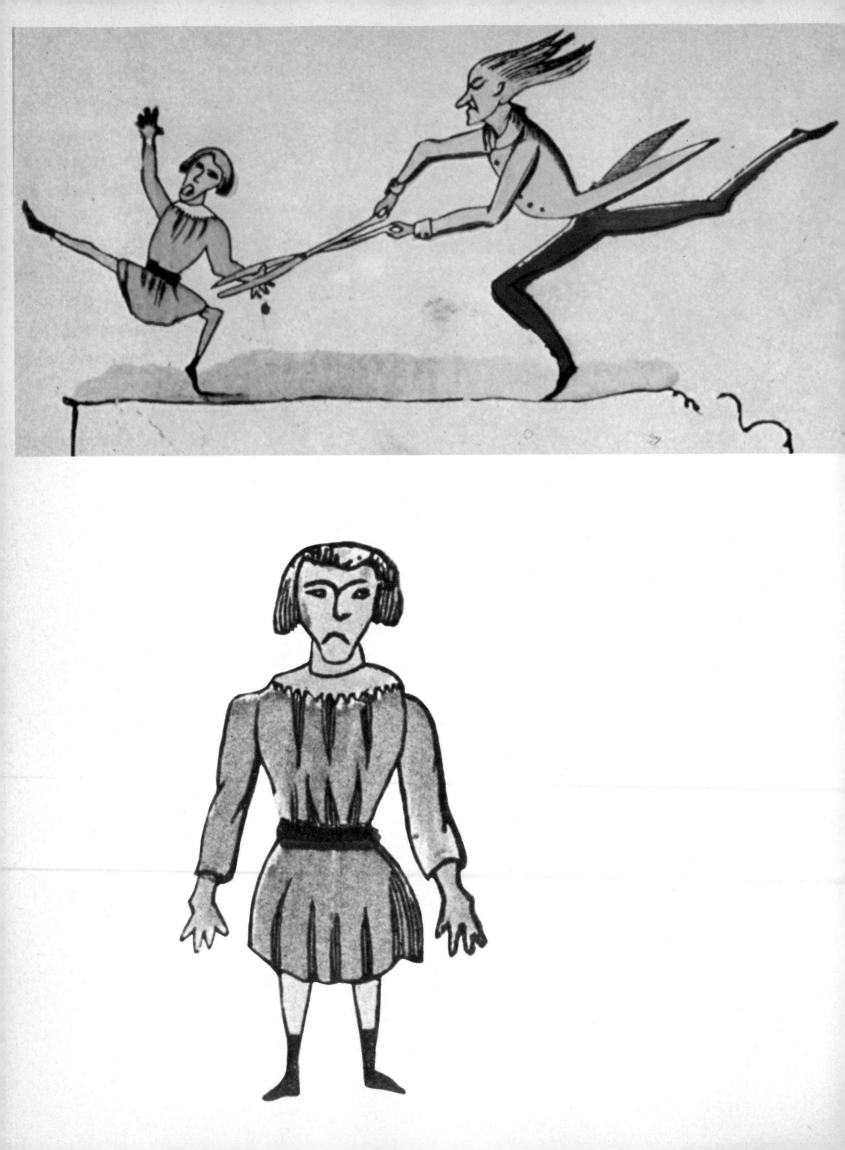

Goody Two Shoes is the world's Goldest – and Gonly – perfect child. Thought to be the creation of Oliver Goldsmith, the playwright who wrote *She Stoops to Conquer,* Goody (ABOVE) began life as a caricature of the perfect(ly awful) brownnoser the writers of cautionary tales seemed to think could exist. But the story soon lost its satirical tone in the wash of repeated tellings.

English artist Walter Crane transformed the workaday Goody of an 1850 collection of children's stories into a Pre-Raphaelite beauty (OPPOSITE).

By 1924, Alice Woodward was illustrating a figure from nothing more than a bedtime story (RIGHT).

By 1826, when George Cruikshank published his first book of illustrations, people were ready to laugh. No matter that the children depicted in *Il Pentamerone* (The Story of Stories) (ABOVE RIGHT), in his famous *Comic Alphabet* (ABOVE LEFT & OPPOSITE) and in *German Popular Stories* (BELOW) were simply shorter adults: that was part of the caricaturist's joke. The joke was all on the grown-ups.

Cruikshank was the first man to make a picture worth a thousand words: until twenty-two of his wondrous etchings appeared in Grimm's *German Popular Stories* (ABOVE & BELOW) in 1823, text and illustration were traditionally strangers to one another. Cruikshank's bulbous, manic characters leavened many a leaden text, but his style–imitated (OPPOSITE) in an etching by John Leech–perfectly complemented Charles Dickens' stories.

Cruikshank's talent is all the more remarkable because he lacked any formal training. His father, himself a painter, died while Cruikshank was a teenager. But having started work as a child of eight, he was by then an established illustrator, and was considered England's greatest satirist by the time he was twenty-five. He lived to be eighty-six.

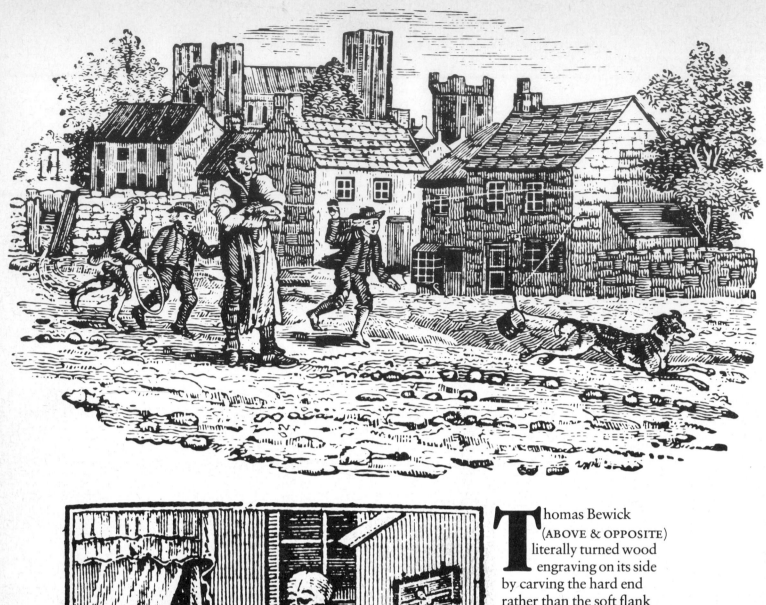

Thomas Bewick (ABOVE & OPPOSITE) literally turned wood engraving on its side by carving the hard end rather than the soft flank of the woodblock. Working directly with only the stamp of his memory, he recreated a childhood spent among the streets and graveyards of Newcastle upon Tyne. An etching by his brother and partner, John Bewick, is shown (LEFT).

It was Thomas, however, who in the course of his lifetime transformed woodcutting from an obscure hobby into an art form. His work, intensely warm and completely personal, embodied an openness that both William Wordsworth and Thomas Carlyle praised (ABOVE & RIGHT).

Nearly fifty years later, Kate Greenaway and Randolph Caldecott would become famous trying to recapture the amusing, rustic innocence of Bewick's scenes from pre-industrial England.

Dick Whittington is literature's most gumptious lad; Jack and Jill its most unlucky couple. Their stories often appeared in the chapbooks of the late eighteenth and early nineteenth centuries. Both tales are parables of lost innocence and, in Whittington's case, virtue and perseverance rewarded. The illustrations on this page are of Dick Whittington at various stages in his journey.

The moral tone of the Jack and Jill story is gentler from repeated tellings. The illustrations shown here are from an early version in which the couple were severely punished upon their return home.

Nonsense, of course, makes more sense. Especially when it is the nonsense of Edward Lear, the famous 'Derry down Derry who loved to see little folks merry.'

A serious illustrator of birds in his unrhyming life, Lear is nonetheless best known for the limericks of love – the nonsense books – he composed and illustrated for the young Edward Stanley, fifteenth earl of Derby, and his playmates. It was for these children, dear to Lear's heart, that the owl and the pussy cat went to sea in that beautiful pea green boat.

The illustrations by Edward Lear are from *The Book of Nonsense to Which is Added More Nonsense*. They are wonderfully redolent of Lear's and the children's mutual need for attention, even when a man in a very large fur coat frightens his young friends (OVERLEAF).

Lear has no qualms about admitting to that need: as the limerick accompanying the book's title page illustration made clear,

'There was an Old Derry
    down Derry,
who loved to see little
    folks merry,
So he made them a Book,
    and with laughter
    they shook
At the fun of that
    Derry down Derry.'

To be read? Nay, not so!...Say rather to be thumbed, to be cooed over, to be dog's-eared, to be rumpled, to be kissed by the illiterate, ungrammatical, dimpled Darlings.' So wrote Lewis Carroll in the introduction to his ultimate childhood fantasy, *Adventures in Wonderland*, first published in 1865. The book was meticulously illustrated by John Tenniel, a brilliant *Punch* satirist who drew

almost entirely from memory and with one eye, having lost the other in a childhood fencing match. Tenniel's matter-of-fact drawings (OPPOSITE BOTTOM, RIGHT & OVERLEAF) beautifully express Alice's every mood, from her horror to her hatred to her delight: they are the standards few subsequent illustrators of the *Alice* books have surpassed. One exception is Ralph Steadman, the contemporary English artist whose bizarre line drawings (BELOW & OPPOSITE ABOVE) are, as Alice would say, 'curiouser and curiouser.'

But Alice is far too intriguing—not to mention demanding—to be dismissed by one or several illustrators. The words of her story seem to remain the same, but seen through the eyes of Gwynedd Hudson (OPPOSITE), Mervyn Peake (LEFT) and Graham Ovenden (BELOW), she is three entirely different people. Just as Lewis Carroll thought in the first place.

Charm has a fragile essence, no sooner effective than overworked. Yet Kate Greenaway, the hugely popular illustrator of the late 1800s, managed to tread the fine line well.

A fueling member of the Arts and Crafts movement along with designer William Morris and illustrator Walter Crane, Greenaway's work benefited from Edmund Evans' improvements to color printing methodology. The success of her career was guaranteed with the 1878 publication of *Under the Window,* a collection of her poems and drawings.

As soon as *Under the Window* appeared, England underwent a Greenaway craze. The first twenty thousand copies of the book sold out immediately. Soon thousands of English schoolchildren sported the quaint period clothes Greenaway drew. Imitators abounded.

Charming, even overly nice and contrived, real life it was not. But neither was the academic drawing against which Greenaway and the other members of the Arts and Crafts movement had reacted. Even her attempt at a Struwwelpeter-type character (OPPOSITE) makes clear that this was a mind and an age that wanted to forgive. Greenaway also drew for *Little Wide Awake,* 'An Illustrated Magazine for Good Children,' whose frontispiece Primrose and Prissy (OVERLEAF) occasionally graced.

A less accomplished draftsman than Greenaway, but as spontaneous as Walter Crane, Randolph Caldecott recognized the energy of a child's fantasies and gave them room to roam. Caldecott's picture book illustrations, with his initials lightly worked into the scenes, are sometimes nearly indistinguishable from Greenaway's. Something of a tragic figure when he died in 1886 at the age of forty, Caldecott was one of the first of a movement that could no longer ignore the personality of a child, and his drawings reflect a spontaneous concern.

The frightened couple (RIGHT & BELOW) adorn the Caldecott version of *The Babes in the Wood,* a traditional tale with an unhappy ending. Caldecott wasn't afraid to confront his young readers with sadness, nor did he hesitate to portray them as the innocently unconcerned tykes they appear to be in this bedside picture (OPPOSITE TOP).

As a child, Caldecott was a sickly boy. Perhaps that is why he celebrates earnestness and energy in his drawing of a baby erupting with enthusiasm for his dinner (OPPOSITE BELOW).

SORE SICKE THEY WERE
AND LIKE TO DYE

Revolution in an industrial society is generally a tame affair: the requirements of material comfort make one think twice about rebelling. Britain's cultural uprising of the 1860s and 1870s took place behind such a curtain, and found its expression in the spread of education.

P. Cruikshank's wonderfully absurd *Comic Alphabet,* from which these examples are taken, was one of the better commercial spellers.

Though commercial, the immensely successful *Chatterbox* and *Little Folks* periodicals of the late nineteenth century played straight to the boiling imaginations of children who were seldom seen and never heard. The emotional repression of Victorian society lurks in every line of the dark etchings, leaking subliminal thoughts. There were plenty of entrepreneurs ready to take advantage of a society that had fallen in love with its 'feelings.'

Chatterbox characters played in mounds of snow (ABOVE) and traveled to strange lands (RIGHT), but the real life children of London had to make do with the magazine and other less active, indoor pursuits. The amorphous sensuality of Victorian children is particularly clear in the portrait of 'Master Mischievous' (OPPOSITE).

Sentiment chafes only when it slops over into sentimentality, and that was very much the case with many of the covers drawn for *Chatterbox* magazine in the 1880s (OVERLEAF).

Dressing up. Snowball wars. Armies of tin. So many children's games imitate the activities of adults. The charm of being someone else is felt early and, from the other side of adulthood, ends late. Yet playing demands even the most temporary freedom from responsibility, and it was this the Victorians were so unwilling to grant their children. Because they published the work of illustrators like Kate Greenaway, Randolph Caldecott and Walter Crane, periodicals such as *Little Wide Awake, Little Foxes* and *Chatterbox* did their part in a battle to re-establish the legitimacy of so private a place as childhood.

The illustrations on these pages are by a few of the many anonymous contributors to the magazines.

People were ready in 1863 for Charles Kingsley's tale of exploration and imagination, *The Water Babies*.

Four years earlier Charles Darwin's *Origin of Species* had sold out on its first day of publication, popularizing the fertile mysteries that could be found in the life unfolding at the ocean's edge. Kingsley's soggy little heroes were amphibious, and combined the innocent freedom of infant water nymphs with the natural inquisitiveness of Darwin himself. They wandered freely above and below the water, bringing their readers information and adventure.

A few of the artists who pictured the infants beneath the blue were Jessie Wilcox Smith (OPPOSITE) who took an ethereal, romantic approach, Heath Robinson (LEFT & BOTTOM) and Linley Sambourne (RIGHT), who favored a Gothic-tinged realism.

The best known depictions of the lagoon creatures are those by Heath Robinson, the brightest light of Great Britain's leading family of book illustrators at the turn of the century.

It is 1864. The notion of an individual artistic personality has been smoldering for nearly a century. Not since Blake have individual tastes emerged sharply out of the cloying smog of academic mindlessness to suggest that perhaps, just perhaps, form has something to do with function.

When the eruption finally came, Walter Crane and his unmistakable imprint were there to give it color, shape and visual humor. Crane used the vivid colors dear to the Pre-Raphaelites and demonstrates an affinity for

And, as the door stood open, in walked boldly,
  This child, whose name was Silverlocks, I'm
There was nobody there to treat her coldly, [told;
  No friend to call her back, no nurse to scold.
She found herself within a parlour charming;
  And there upon the table there were placed
Three basins, sending up a smell so warming,
  That she at once felt hungry, and must taste.
The largest basin first, but hot and biting
  The soup was in it, and the second too;
The smallest basin tasted so inviting,
  That up she ate it all, with small ado.

Japanese colorprints in his work. The result was the decoration of the human spirit. Crane believed a child could see everything the artist saw: to prove the point, he made money selling richly produced 'toy books' for sixpence. A child's body houses the free spirit of a bird. It deserves setting free, for in Crane's view, you are what you see.

(OVERLEAF), a Pre-Raphaelite family gathers in a garden.

Who taught my infant lips to pray,
And love God's holy book and day,
And walk in Wisdom's pleasant way?
My Mother

And can I ever cease to be
Affectionate and kind to thee,

Who was so very kind to me,
    My Mother?

Ah, no! the thought I cannot fear;
And if God please my life to spare,
I hope I shall reward thy care,
    My Mother

The alphabet shown here is from one of Crane's most beautiful toy books, *The Alphabet of Old Friends.* Crane is remembered most for his near perfect sense of design, but his sense of humor was just as well developed.

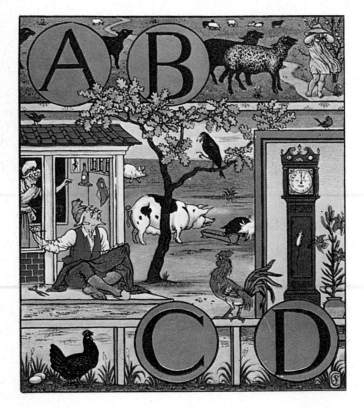

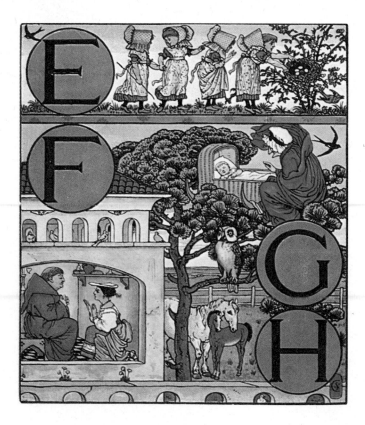

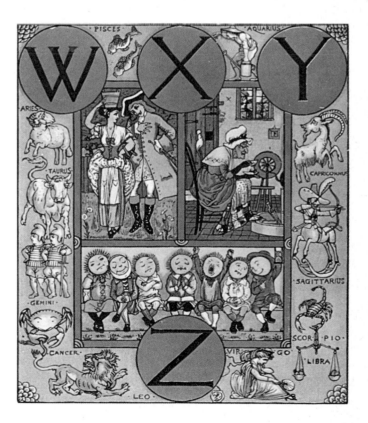

'Goblin Market' is the poem that established the reputation of the Pre-Raphaelite school of poetry when it was published in 1862. Perverse, intensely erotic, repressed, guilty and hinting at incest, 'Goblin Market' reveals the secret psychological life of its retiring author, Christina Rossetti, as she relates the adventures of two sisters tempted by goblins in the woods. Many illustrators have tried to plumb the labyrinthine fantasies of the poem, but none have succeeded like those artists whose styles are sinewy and secretive. One of the poem's first illustrators was Christina's brother, Dante Gabriel Rossetti (ABOVE). Later, Laurence Housman (LEFT) amplified the poem's evil tone, as did its most famous realizer, Arthur Rackham (OPPOSITE).

The responsibility of a providing parent. And the weightlessness of being a child.

It is this contrast that adults carry most wistfully and makes them insist that youth is wasted on the young.

It was the same longing that moved E.V. Lucas in 1900 to write a book of children's verse called *Four and Twenty Toilers*. He was no stranger to publication, having already established himself as essayist, journalist, editor and art historian.

Lucas took his place in children's literature with the help of Francis Bedford, the lucid and gifted illustrator, who brought the children to life.

It was Bedford who magically juxtaposed a child's infirmity of purpose with a laborer's dogged industry, who threw the fancy and caprice of youth against the relief of grown-up persistence and plodding.

It is curious that mankind chooses youth as the time for compulsory education, thus ensuring a remarkable conformity of thought in adult years.

All over the globe, children between the ages of six and sixteen are persuaded and taught, instilled with beliefs and opinions. They enter the kingdom of books and become collectors of knowledge, much of which will be inapplicable in a later world.

Yet somehow through the system of instruction comes enlightenment and reason – sometimes from the classroom and sometimes at the knee of one older and wiser.

Shown here are a seventeenth-century classroom from *Orbis Pictus* by Johann Comenius (OPPOSITE TOP), a befuddled baby by Linley Sambourne (OPPOSITE MIDDLE) and a scene of numeric confusion by Walter Crane (OPPOSITE BOTTOM).

Another of F.D. Bedford's detailed illustrations from *Four and Twenty Toilers* (TOP) shows the bedlam and refreshment of school children. Reginald Marsh's wispy students are hard at it (MIDDLE), while Tom Brown and his friends relax in a quadrangle scene by Hugh Thomson (BOTTOM).

But school would be pleasant without punishment, and that just wouldn't do: thus, the art of the reprimand. Edward Ardizzone's reclining boys are about to catch it (ABOVE), but for the scapegoats in *Chatterbox* (BELOW LEFT), *The Good Child's Reward* (BELOW RIGHT) and on the cover of *Collier's* magazine (OPPOSITE), it is a moment too late.

School yards seem to invite high emotions and fisticuffs. Perhaps it is only by physical action that one can keep abstract knowledge in perspective. Or perhaps it is simply the nature of little boys. And little girls.

Grace Floyd drew the young ladies' tug-of-war (OPPOSITE BELOW), and the skirmish (BELOW) was sketched by an unsigned contributor to *Chatterbox*. In Tomi Ungerer's depiction of sibling affection, Little Brother seems to be on the losing end of things (OPPOSITE TOP).

The donnybrook of cherubic boys (OVERLEAF) was drawn by Jacques Stella.

There is no sense of wonderment greater than that of a child on a journey. Whether a fugitive, a tourist, a pilgrim or an adventurer, it matters not. A change of locale excites the mind.

It sometimes excites the tongue, too, to the point where the tales of a traveler become fabulous and vulnerable to exaggeration. Freedom to a storyteller is the absence of witnesses.

Huckleberry Finn was a young wayfarer who knew how to stretch the truth when in the right company. E.W. Kemble's sketch from the original 1885 publication shows Huck lying low in his canoe, dodging his father and the townspeople, scheming a story as he drifts downriver (LEFT).

Arthur Rackham takes us from the rustic Mississippi Valley to the skyline of London as Peter Pan steps out for the evening. This drawing is from the original 1906 *Peter Pan in Kensington Gardens* (ABOVE).

Shown (OPPOSITE) is an illustration of a family ferry excursion across the English channel by Thomas Crane, Walter Crane's brother.

Among the more delicious feelings shared by children are the twin delights of secrecy and conspiracy. Silence and shared confidence heighten the senses.

Few illustrators have been better equipped to portray these feelings than the prolific Swedish graphic artist Carl Larsson. He rarely strayed from his own hearth, from where he constantly observed and painted his family.

His detailed watercolors caught the enigmas and mysteries of his children, such as their bold curiosity on Christmas Eve, 1892 (OPPOSITE).

The other secrets shared here are Walter Crane's sketch of the stealthy girl in *Carrots* (ABOVE), published in 1846, and 'Ruth's Secret' (LEFT) from the Victorian magazine *Little Wide Awake*.

One of the master draftsmen of the early twentieth century was the French-born Edmund Dulac. By the time he became a British subject at the age of thirty, he already ranked with Arthur Rackham as a leading luxury book illustrator.

Best known for his fairy-tale studies, he betrayed Middle Eastern and Oriental influences in much of his work. Shown (OPPOSITE) is a sample of his work from *Stories from Hans Andersen*.

The Dulac illustration (ABOVE) is a more frivolous caricature from *Lyrics Pathetic and Humorous,* depicting a Japanese child saddened by the butterfly taking a nap on her flower.

There is a suspended quality in Arthur Rackham's work, a dense, atmospheric feeling. One feels that, could one but shake the scene, the foggy mood would precipitate.

It was this stylized use of half-light in settings of deformed trees and weather-beaten urban structures that made Rackham the giant of early twentieth-century illustrators. His fair-skinned children hid and played in the shadows of these surroundings, giving the pictures a Gothic tension.

Rackham's work includes *Peter Pan* (LEFT & ABOVE), *Rip Van Winkle*, *Alice in Wonderland*, *Grimms' Fairy Tales*, *Aesop's Fables*, *A Christmas Carol* and Edgar Allen Poe's *Tales of Mystery and Imagination*.

Some more illustrations by Arthur Rackham, the great subliminal Victorian. The child on crutches – a common sight even in Rackham's day – is from an edition of Robert Browning's *Pied Piper of Hamelin*. Peter Pan (OP-POSITE) sails on a stream in Kensington Park while his earthbound friends (ABOVE LEFT) chase leaves. Later (ABOVE RIGHT) he takes advice from old Solomon Caw.

The team of Maud and Miska Petersham illustrated dozens of books, and their appealing drawings, with their superb linear technique and bold, almost Slavic colors, were as arresting as any text. The illustrations here are from *The Poppyseed Cakes,* published in the early 1920s.

Carl Sandburg is generally remembered as a poet, as a Pulitzer prize-winning biographer or as a folksinger. The populist American poet also wrote several volumes of children's literature, one of which, *Rootabaga Stories,* was illustrated by the Petershams (BELOW). The other illustrations here (LEFT & OPPOSITE) are from *The Poppyseed Cakes.*

One of the lasting romantic stereotypes is the healthy and mischievous provincial child. The children themselves may be no more innocently portrayed than in Arthur Rackham's work, but in these pictures, the harmony is rooted in the lush rural setting. Perfect examples of that harmony abound in the work of Thomas Hart Benton, the American painter who died in 1975 at the age of eighty-five. He was a master of the parochial image, as seen (ABOVE) in 'The Music Lesson,' painted in 1943. Benton strove for a vision of America, and he found it in detail – in this case, a young girl's rapt attention, her doll and her bare feet.

Benton's contemporary and Canadian counterpart, Paul Peel, worked in the same style. Shown (OPPOSITE) is his oil painting 'The Young Biologist,' 1891. Scientific principles – and a good, plump frog – are clearly at hand.

By the twentieth century the child was for sale. The related expansions of technology and commercialism pushed illustration to a wider market and its publication assumed new and precise motives.

In some cases, like the cornstarch poster (RIGHT), the new technology served to resurrect the old. It is a British woodcut poster from 1900, partially set in the old woodcut traditions, and partially serving as a forerunner of the modern posters, with their clear outlines and large expanses of solid color.

Although the poster is signed 'J and W. Beggarstaff,' it is the work of Sir William Nicholson and James Pryde, two graphic artists who clearly did not want to be associated with creeping commercialism.

Examples of technology for its own sake. Published in a book titled *Magic Moments,* the first picture (RIGHT) changes into the second (BELOW) at the tug of a string. The sketches are by Florence Hardy.

CINÉMATOGRAPHE LUMIÈRE

The sophisticated poster printing techniques of the French continued to produce state-of-the-arts advertising posters (ABOVE & OPPOSITE). British techniques were less adventurous (RIGHT). But the end result was still the same: these posters were designed not to enlighten, but to sell. Inevitably, advertising's children were happier, more wholesome and always far plumper and healthier than their counterparts in real life.

"Waiting for PEARS."

A part of an alphabet and other 'childhood scenes' used in French advertisements at the turn of the century when children had a potent, if mindlessly exploited, commercial image.

William Heath Robinson, son and grandson of engravers, fresh out of art school, turned away from his aspirations of a painter's life to the bread-and-butter pursuit of illustration. By the age of twenty-four, the young man was happily married, and was never again out of work.

Although best known for his absurd and comic parodies of seemingly ordinary situations, he was also a very evocative and eloquent illustrator of serious works. The Wild Man (BELOW) is from his 1912 collection of stories about a boot cleaner named Bill who became a 'minder,' baby-sitter to a large flock of children. After much adventure, the companions manage to restore the eccentric King of Troy to his throne. Robinson was also a master of the inspired silhouette (BOTTOM).

Winsor McCay, born two years after Robinson in 1871, took advantage of the very special place that dreams evoke. In his newspaper comic strip, 'Little Nemo in Slumberland' (OPPOSITE), which first appeared in the *New York Herald* in 1905, McCay's imagination and pen ran wild as Nemo dreamed of comic police chases, talking animals and of growing almost larger than the world. At the end of each day's strip, Little Nemo would awaken, having fallen out of bed.

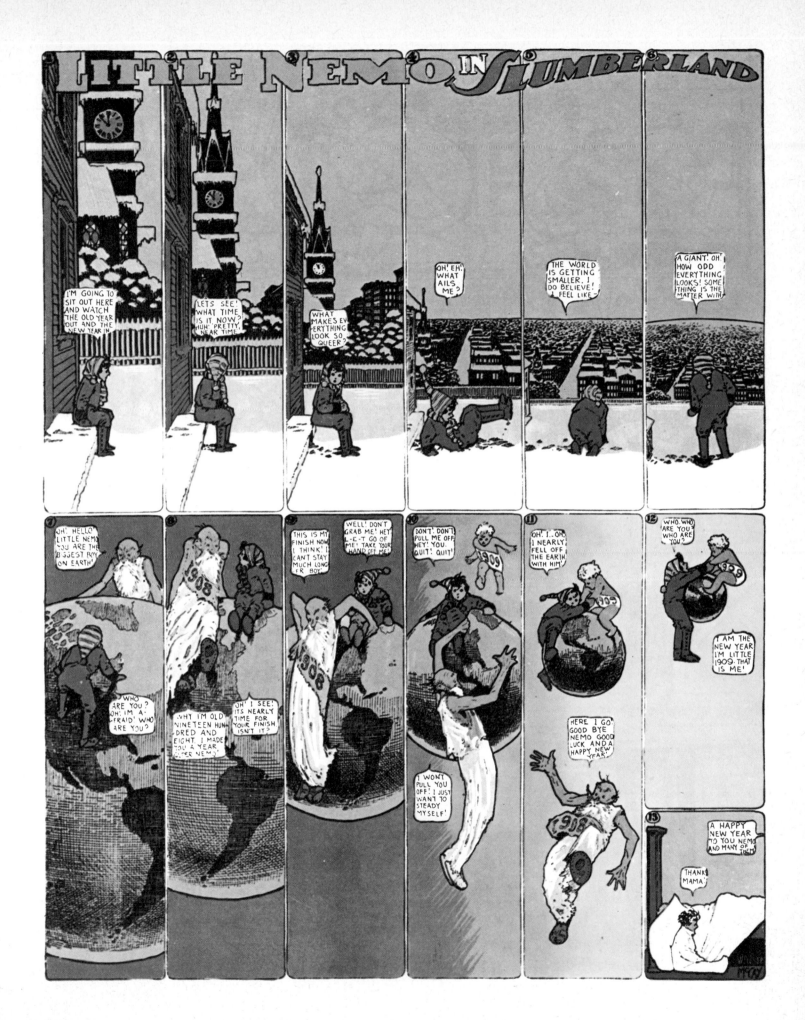

Two contempo-
raries of Robinson
were W.W. Den-
slow, who illus-
trated *The Wizard of Oz*
(OPPOSITE), and Winnie-
the-Pooh artist Ernest
Shepard, whose work here
(BELOW) is from *The Reluc-
tant Dragon*. Simple lines,
simple drawings, powerful
effect.

The first comic to hit it big was The Katzenjammer Kids, created by Rudolph Dirk in 1897 and adapted to the stage by 1903. The two rebellious twins, Hans and Fritz, took great delight in defying all types of authority (RIGHT & BELOW).

In 1914 the strip was taken over by Harold Knerr, who turned it into a continuous classic until his death in 1949. It was unsuccessfully revived by two other artists in the 1950s.

The hero of the very first comic strip, published in a New York newspaper in 1895, was a child. His name was Yellar Kid. He wore a long nightshirt on which the artist, R.F. Outcault, would print messages to his readers (LEFT).

The Yellar Kid, an Oriental-looking child, provoked a mild racist debate among the city's liberal intelligentsia. Embarrassed by his own creation, Outcault terminated the comic strip after three years.

One other durable child who was a star in the comics before she came to Broadway was Little Orphan Annie. Created in 1924 by Harold Gray as the heroine of comicland's first morality plays and parables, she became famous for her empty eyes and wisdom beyond her years (CENTRE LEFT).

Little Orphan Annie died in 1968 at the same age as when she was created. Swee' Pea (BOTTOM) lives on as Popeye's youngest, wisest companion.

American illustration came into its own in the twentieth century and Hugh Lofting, who illustrated his own Dr. Dolittle stories, became the toast of the 1920s.

Using simple, guileless line drawings, Lofting's strength was composition. He was able to suggest substance and depth with the lightest of pencil strokes. Shown (OPPOSITE TOP) is an illustration from *The Voyage of Doctor Dolittle.*

American illustration after Lofting includes the work of Garth Williams in E.B. White's *Charlotte's Web* (BELOW), and Robert McCloskey's stories that introduced the world to the well-intentioned but disaster-prone Homer Price (OPPOSITE BOTTOM).

To Maxfield Parrish, the preeminent American illustrator at the turn of this century, memories of childhood were practically dreams, excursions into a subconscious past without any fixed destination. Dreams suggested night to Parrish, and night meant the predominant use of shadows even in his posters (BELOW). But it was in his illustrations for poetry that Parrish really indulged his taste for fantasy, as the painting 'Seein' Things' (OPPOSITE) – done for Eugene Field's *Poem of Childhood* – makes abundantly clear.

More and more children appeared in advertisements as more and more advertisers recognized the commercial appeal of innocence.

Somehow cleanliness figured within the equation too, though very few children, innocent or otherwise, stay clean for long. Nevertheless, children featured prominently in both the British Pears soap advertisement by John Everett Millais (OVERLEAF LEFT) and another advertisement for soap by Frances Tipton Hunter (OVERLEAF RIGHT).

What book, what illustration, what childhood is not, after all, a dream? Jaunts through innocence and fantasy, dreams are part of the lives of adults and children alike. Adults simply make the mistake of taking them less seriously and considering them less real.

Children know better. Little Nemo took his creator Winsor McCay through Slumberland every night, only to fall out of bed in the morning (RIGHT) onto the pages of the *New York Herald.* Emil, drawn in the 1920s by Walter Trier, has the same trouble controlling his nocturnal wanderings (OPPOSITE).

(LEFT), the hero of *My Father's Dragon* takes an all-too-real ride from a rhinoceros, and W.W. Denslow is just sending Dorothy off to Oz (BELOW).

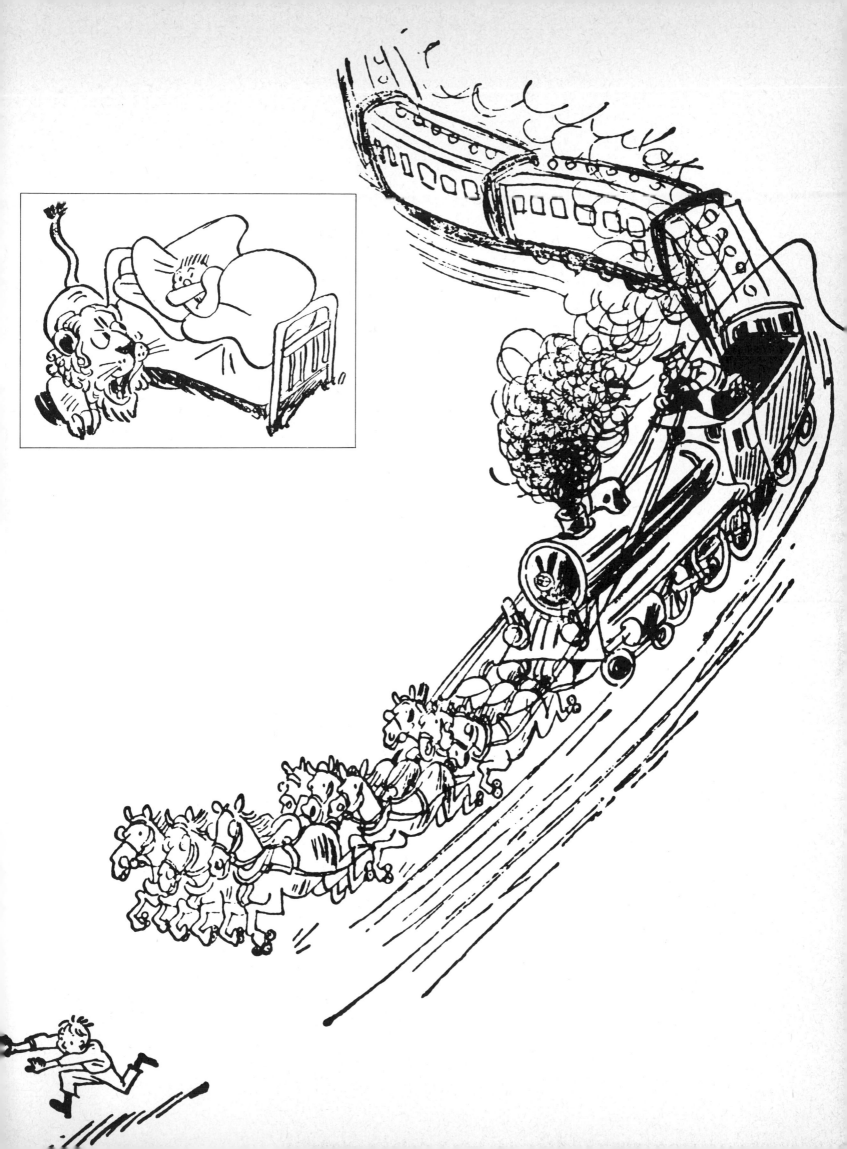

Happily, the course of children's illustration has broadened with time. Illustrators today create amazing new worlds at every stroke of the pen. That is as it should be: the imagination deserves no bounds. Yet each illustrator does it differently. Maurice Sendak's young boy inhabits a world of diffuse awareness (OPPOSITE BELOW).

The Great Brain (OPPOSITE ABOVE), from Mercer Mayer's *More Adventures of the Great Brain,* deals in hard currency, notably ingeniousness.

Victoria Chess and Edward Gorey set Zenobia (of *Fletcher and Zenobia*) up in a tree (ABOVE & LEFT). There she is found by Fletcher, a racoon who holds a party in her honor. A moth comes to spend the night, and grows rather larger than anyone had expected.

anadian illustrator Heather Cooper seems to wonder just how real childhood is to anyone but a child: it is a world unto itself that excludes even a child's parents. Cooper found solace from being left out by painting a version of her daughter's daydreams (LEFT). For Sarah on the beach (OPPOSITE), adult proportions are entirely inappropriate. In her line drawing (BELOW), Cooper explores the power of the childish imagination: how can so much fit into those tiny heads?

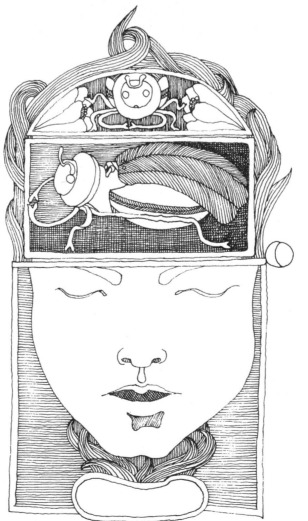

There is something particularly English about the illustrations of Edward Ardizzone, easily the country's most prolific illustrator.

Yet the effect has more to it than scenery. His characters are always finding themselves thrust into eventful situations and his drawings, like any child performing heroics, are full of unassuming grace, spontaneous color and charged emotion. The pictures here are from his book, *Mimff Takes Charge*.

Ardizzone's first *Little Tim* book was published in 1936, and some dozen others have appeared since. Ardizzone's quietly spontaneous, unfussed sketches perfectly capture the emotional nuances of the plucky Tim's experiences: the rummy warmth of Captain McFee's fireside stories (ABOVE) and childhood camaraderie (OPPOSITE ABOVE).

Next to Ardizzone the wholesome and wholesale realism of Norman Rockwell shouts out loud: his is a young boy's America (RIGHT).